For Kevin McCarthy—D.D.M.

To the Reader: May you find love in your everyday life.—C.G.

© 2005 Dandi Daley Mackall.

© 2005 Standard Publishing, Cincinnati, Ohio.

A division of Standex International Corporation.

All rights reserved. Printed in China.

Project editor: Robin Stanley.

Cover and interior design: Marissa Bowers.

Scripture quotations are taken from The Holy Bible, New Living Translation, copyright © 1996.

Used by permission of Tyndale House Publishers, Inc., Wheaton, IL. 60189.

All rights reserved.

12 11 10 09 08 07 06 05   9 8 7 6 5 4 3 2 1

Library of Congress Cataloging-in-Publication Data

Mackall, Dandi Daley.

The best thing is love / written by Dandi Daley Mackall ; pictures by Claudine Gévry.

p. cm. -- (My favorite verses)

ISBN 0-7847-1532-7 (case bound picture book)

1. Bible. N.T. 1 Corinthians XIII--Paraphrases, English--Juvenile literature.

I. Gévry, Claudine. II. Title. III. Series: Mackall, Dandi Daley. My favorite verses

BS2677.M23 2005   227'.20520834--dc22   2004017952

We all need faith and hope but THE BEST THING IS LOVE

Written by Dandi Daley Mackall

Pictures by Claudine Gévry

STANDARD PUBLISHING
CINCINNATI, OHIO

If I talk all fancy,
or I sing in rhyme,

But I don't have love, it's a waste of time.
Then I'm not much better
than a clanging chime.

Love

The very best thing is love.

If I could speak in any language...but didn't love others, I would only be making meaningless nois

1 Corinthians 13:1

If I knew the future, they might make me king!
I could build a castle; I'd know everything.
Still, I'd need real love only God can bring . . .

Love

The very best thing is love.

If I knew all the mysteries of the future...but didn't love others, what good would I be?
1 Corinthians 13:2

If my brain's as big as a basketball . . .
The computer breaks? I'm the one you call.
Without love,
I am nothing but a know-it-all.

Love

The very best thing is love.

If I knew...everything about everything, but didn't love others, what good would I be?
1 Corinthians 13:2

If I had the faith that I know I could,
and I cried, "Move, mountain!"
and it really would,
but I don't show love, then my faith's no good.

Love

The very best thing is love.

If I had the gift of faith so that I could speak to a mountain and make it move, without love I would be no good to anybody.

1 Corinthians 13:2

With a big allowance,
I could feed the poor.

But the chances are that I would still want more.
Without love, my gift is just another chore.

The very best thing is love.

If I gave everything I have to the poor...I could boast about it; but if I didn't love others, I would be of no value whatsoever.

1 Corinthians 13:3

God says love is patient;
God says love is kind.
But a love like that is very hard to find.
What I need is Jesus in my heart and mind.

Love

The very best thing is love.

Love is patient and kind.

1 Corinthians 13:4

If I'm glad when others
can do something great,
if I'm still okay
when I have to wait,

T hen I just might
have a cause to celebrate.

Love

The very best thing is love.

Love is not jealous or boastful or proud or rude. Love does not demand its own way.
1 Corinthians 13:4

Love is always honest, never tells a lie.
Love just won't give up;
love will always try.
Love will give a break to the other guy.

Love

The very best thing is love.

All our bikes will rust.
All our toys will break.

Only love will last, love for Jesus' sake.
When we go to heaven, love is all we'll take.

The very best thing is love.

Love will last forever.

1 Corinthians 13:8

I won't know too much on this earthly place.
But when I'm in heaven, only by God's grace,
I'll ask God for answers.
We'll be face to face.

Love

The very best thing is love.

All that I know now is partial and incomplete, but then I will know everything completely, just as God knows me now.

1 Corinthians 13:12

Now we all need faith. (God is out of sight!)
And we must have hope; it's our guiding light.
But what God wants most,
and you know it's right . . .

Love

The very best thing is love.

1 Corinthians 13

¹If I could speak in any language in heaven or on earth but didn't love others, I would only be making meaningless noise like a loud gong or a clanging cymbal. ²If I had the gift of prophecy, and if I knew all the mysteries of the future and knew everything about everything, but didn't love others, what good would I be? And if I had the gift of faith so that I could speak to a mountain and make it move, without love I would be no good to anybody. ³If I gave everything I have to the poor and even sacrificed my body, I could boast about it; but if I didn't love others, I would be of no value whatsoever.

For you!

⁴Love is patient and kind. Love is not jealous or boastful or proud ⁵or rude. Love does not demand its own way. Love is not irritable, and it keeps no record of when it has been wronged. ⁶It is never glad about injustice but rejoices whenever the truth wins out. ⁷Love never gives up, never loses faith, is always hopeful, and endures through every circumstance.